Understanding Boat Plumbing and Water Systems

Understanding Boat Plumbing and Water Systems

JOHN C. PAYNE

SHERIDAN HOUSE

This edition first published 2008 by
Sheridan House Inc.
145 Palisade Street,
Dobbs Ferry, NY 10522
www.sheridanhouse.com

Library of Congress Cataloging-In-Publication Data
Payne, John C.
     Understanding boat plumbing and water systems / John C. Payne.
        p. cm.
     Includes index.
     ISBN 978-1-57409-263-9 (pbk. : alk. paper)
        1. Boats and boating—Maintenance and repair. 2. Plumbing—
     Repairing. I. Title.

     VM322.P58 2008
     623.8'54—dc22   2008017852

Printed in the United States of America

ISBN 978-1-57409-263-9

CONTENTS

1. BOAT PLUMBING SYSTEMS

Modern sailing and motor boats have several water systems that must be properly planned, installed and maintained. A failure in a sewage system can make life very uncomfortable when you are out on the water; in the gray water system, such as the shower drain and the sink, a breakdown is at best very inconvenient. A stoppage in the bilge water system is dangerous and virtually renders your boat unseaworthy; in the fresh water system it can make life very hard until you reach shore. Fresh water is absolutely essential, and having the capacity to make it rather than finding ports and marinas to refill increases ranges and cruising options.

What are the standards?

A boat owner should comply with local national standards.

1. **ABYC H-23 — Installation of Potable Water Systems for Use on Boats.** These are voluntary technical practices and engineering standards for the design, construction, and installation of potable water supply systems on boats.

2. **ABYC H-22 — Electric Bilge Pump Systems.** The standards for the design, construction, installation, operation, and control of electric bilge pump systems apply to all boats equipped with electric bilge pump systems.

2. FRESH WATER SYSTEMS

Fresh water systems include the drinking or potable water supply and storage system, and the shower and galley water system. A typical pressurized water system arrangement is illustrated below. Look at Jabsco (www.jabsco.com) who also own FloJet and Rule. You can also check Whale at www.whalepumps.com. The water system schematic is supplied courtesy of Cleghorn Waring (www.cleghorn.co.uk)

Figure 2-1 Pressurized Water System
(Courtesy Cleghorn Waring)

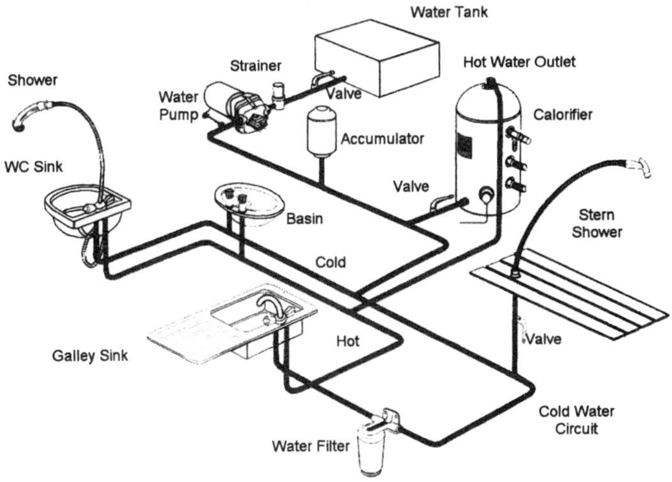

Water storage tanks

Tanks have traditionally been manufactured from stainless steel. The increasing use of thick walled high-density polyethylene tanks is now becoming very common. They have less leak and corrosion problems than stainless steel tanks and are much lighter. Some boats may also use flexible water bladders, that are suitable for non-standard shapes and areas.

The basic storage system consists of one or two water tanks, a water filler cap on deck with 1½-inch reinforced hose to the tank. There is also a ½-inch vent overflow that uses reinforced hose to the upper part of the hull with an overboard fitting. This allows air to escape when filling with the water and for water to flow overboard when the tank is full.

Tank monitoring

The monitoring of onboard water and bilge levels is an essential task. A simple electrical gauge can be installed that provides the necessary information.

Resistance Type Tank Sensors. The majority of tank sensors operate by varying a resistance proportional to the tank level contents. The two basic sensor types are:

1. **Immersion Pipe Type.** This sensor type consists of a damping tube, with an internal float that moves up and down along two wires. These units are only suitable for fuel tanks. The big advantage with these sensor types is that they are well damped and therefore fluctuating readings are virtually eliminated.

2. **Lever Type.** The lever type system consists of a sensor head located on the end of an adjustable leg. The sensor head comprises a variable resistance and float arm pivot. As the float arm moves relative to fluid levels, the resistance alters and the meter reading changes. Typical resistance readings are in the range 10–180 Ohms. Lever type units should be installed longitudinally, as athwartships orientation can cause serious problems with the vessel rolling.

Capacitive Type Tank Sensors. This type of transducer operates on the principle that the value of a capacitor is dependent on the dielectric between plates. The sender unit measures the capacitance difference between air and the liquid.

1. **Output Values.** The sensing circuit outputs a voltage proportional to the level in the typical range of 0 to 5 volts.

2. **Faults.** The most common fault in these systems is water damage to the circuit board, usually because of tank condensation.

Pressure Type Sensors. These sensor types are considerably more expensive, but they are very accurate and less prone to damage. The transducers are either placed at the bottom of the tank, or on a pipe that is taken out of the side at the tank bottom. They are more common on larger boat computer based integrated monitoring systems.

1. **Output Values.** The sensors output either a 4–20 milliamps or 0.6–2.6 volts proportional to the pressure of the fluid in the tank. The pressure value is proportional to the tank volume.

2. **Faults.** If the sensor is located on a small pipe it may become clogged.

Tank gauge testing

Use the following procedure on suspected gauge faults.

Open Sensor Test. Remove the sensor lead marked "G" from the back of the gauge. Switch on meter supply voltage. The gauge needle should now be in the right-hand hard-over position.

Sensor Ground Test. This test involves the bridging of sensor input terminal "G" to negative. The sensor lead must be removed and the meter supply on. The gauge needle should now be in the left-hand hard-over position.

Flexible hose

The most common hose used in water systems is the reinforced hose. The hose is reinforced to prevent collapsing due to water suction pressures as well bursting due to water system pressures. Hoses are usually reinforced with a rigid helix or a woven polyester braid. When used in potable water installations the hoses should be high-quality grade approved by the FDA or equivalent as this signifies that it is made from non-toxic compounds. Approved hoses should not be able to support microbiological growth. The hose should have a temperature range to suit both hot and cold water. Piping must be capable of withstanding the water system pressures. For example Whale piping is rated at 60 psi and 90°C.

1. When installing water piping, the longer the run, the larger the pipe that is required. This reduces the friction losses inside the pipe.

2. When installing hose, the runs should be as straight as practicable without any sharp bends or kinks. This causes resistance to water flow.

3. All potable water hoses should be above the bilge. If they are not, thought should be given to contamination or the effects of oil and other bilge water material.

Semi-rigid piping

Manufacturers such as Whale have the Quick Connect system and a color-coded semi-rigid pipe system (i.e. red, blue and green). This piping uses compression fittings to join or terminate. Ensure that the pipe is not kinked, and where tight bends are required install a bend. The system is excellent and I used this on my own boat. To install it, you will need a special cutting tool for preparing the hose ends. Whale also have the WaterWeb system which allows multiple connections with 2 cold and 2 hot water inlets and 7 cold and 5 hot water outlets.

Figure 2-2 Water Web Installation
(Courtesy Whale)

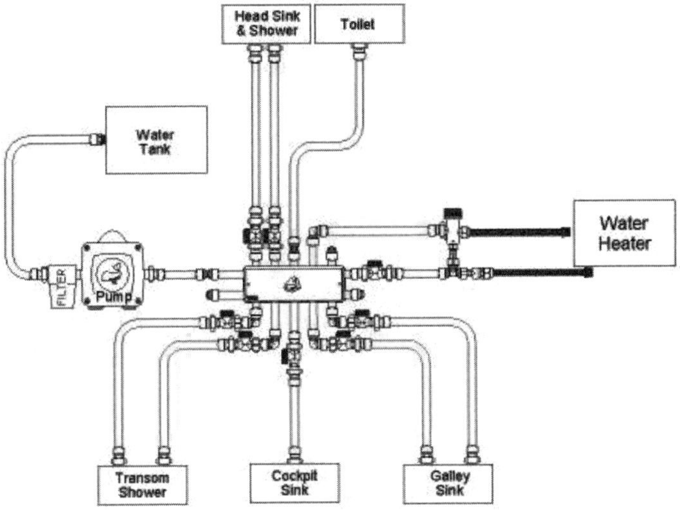

Hose fittings

All water system hose fittings and joints must be capable of withstanding operating pressures (20–50 psi) within the water system. In most systems the hoses are kept pressurized all the time.

Joints must be tight and secure to avoid water pressure leaking off, which causes greater pump cycling. All hoses should be secured using 2 stainless steel worm drive hose clamps. The water pump usually has pipe or hose barbs on the inlet and outlet.

When placing hoses onto barbed fittings it is often easier to place the ends in hot water to soften them up. Make sure you push the hoses on over the entire barb and not half way. In most distribution systems PVC T-joints are installed with stainless steel hose clips. One issue that always comes up is compatibility; in most cases you will need to use reducers or pipe-to-hose barbs for ½-inch ID hoses.

Hose clamps

The worm drive hose clamp is virtually the universal method for securing flexible hoses onto hose tails. They come in a variety of stainless steel and electroplated steel. The cheaper ones tend to corrode very easily when the plated surface is scratched.

1. Always lubricate the worm drive to maximize the clamping force being applied. The higher the pressure and the larger the diameter of the hose the greater the clamping force required.

2. Always use the correct size screwdriver when clamping. Incorrect drivers damage the slot; with undersized drivers you generally cannot achieve the clamping force required.

Valves

There are a variety of valves that can be used on the various boat water systems. Valves are used to isolate either water on or water off, and are not used to regulate or control water. Types of valves in use on a boat include the following:

Tapered Plug Cock

These traditional valves are often cast with an integral flange for mounting against the hull and a threaded inlet designed to receive a through hull fitting. The bore is straight through when in the open position and the closing action will tend to shear any obstruction. The smooth straight bore is important on a sea valve as it is easy to clean and antifoul from outside the hull when out of the water. The position of the handle clearly shows whether the valve is open or closed.

Ball Valves

These valves shave a clear bore and 90 degree action but do not have the same high turning torque. The pierced ball seals against resilient synthetic materials and gives a good seal and lower friction. As a sea valve the bronze Class or UL approved valve is the best available. Plastic ball valves are also available and they are corrosion free. You have to be sure that solvents, such as those in bottom paint and antifouling, cannot affect the material.

Gate Valves

Gate valves require many turns to open and close and have limited uses on a boat. They should not be used as sea valves although they are in some cases.

Check Valves

Non-return or check valves allow flow in one direction only. Most are of the swing type. A hinged disk is pushed out of the way when water flows in the forward direction and swings back to seal against a lip when in the reverse flow condition. The sealing force is usually only provided by the pressure of the water so they can leak in low pressure systems.

Check valves do tend to be unreliable and should not be used in critical systems. Systems must be clean. One cause of failure is debris and material jamming under the flap. They are never an alternative to a proper stop valve or isolation valve in a discharge line.

Through-hull fittings

Through-hull water fittings have several purposes. When used in wood, fiberglass or sandwich constructed boats they seal and protect the hull material where the opening in the hull is made. They also locally reinforce the hull where the hole has potentially weakened it. The fitting distributes the load that is applied to the connected valve. Finally the fitting clamps the valve securely to the hull. While plastic through-hull fittings are common, bronze is much stronger below or near the waterline.

Through-hull problems

In seawater bronze through-hull fittings and valves must be of the highest quality possible. Lower quality bronze fittings can suffer from de-zincification, potentially threatening the boat's safety. The zinc slowly corrodes to leave porous and very brittle copper. Using brass is not the same as using bronze. Quality bronze alloys use minimal zinc and are more resilient to saltwater. Be careful when buying bronze fittings and only install those from reputable suppliers. Don't buy fittings that simply are said to be Naval or Admiralty etc., without supporting documentation.

How to maintain water quality

It is good practice to have at least two separate tanks for stowing water. Before filling a tank, transfer the remaining water to another tank. The new water can be put in the tank without contaminating the known good quality, and if found to be of poor quality and you need to dump it, you do not lose all your water. Toxin levels are generally characterized by unpleasant smells that are created by toxic by-products from bacteria. Cleaning regimes should be undertaken at least twice a year to ensure the integrity of the water.

1. **Tank Cleaning.** The tank should be scoured by hand with a brush, but do not use excessive quantities of detergent.

2. **Tank Flushing.** Fill the tank and flush out at least three times.

3. **Tank Disinfection.** As bacteria are still present and viable, the new water and tank must be disinfected to prevent early re-growth.

More on system disinfection

This is also sometimes called shocking the system. Chlorination of water is easily accomplished by adding a solution of household bleach in the quantities of 5 to 100 of tank contents. Let some amount run though all outlets to disinfect all parts of the system. Top up the water tank and allow to stand for four hours. Re-flush the system another three times.

Another greener method is to pour in a quantity of white vinegar in the ratio of 1 liter to 50 liters of system capacity and allow to stand for 2 days. Refill with fresh water and flush 3 times again. The tank is then ready for use and will maintain potable water quality for several months.

Another easier and quicker way is to use Puriclean or Aquatabs or a similar brand solution, which will clean and purify the tank. After filling the tank and adding the cleaning solution, let it stand for a few hours, then follow by flushing. Remember to always run the solution through all outlets and piping to clean the entire system.

Water pressure pumps

The primary purpose of the water pump is to supply and pressurize the water distribution system from the water tank. A pump is selected based on the number of outlets to be supplied and the flow rate required. If the pump is incorrectly rated for the system the flow will drop off when another outlet is opened. Variable speed pumps are now available from SHURflo and Jabsco that vary the speed to maintain water pressure without the annoying pressure variations on traditional systems.

The diaphragm pump

These units are the most commonly used. They are robust and designed for multi-outlet high pressure water systems. They are more tolerant to dry running conditions, self-priming, and relatively quiet in operation. Pressure switches are usually built into the pump. The older pump types were belt driven by an electric motor. The piston moved a diaphragm up and down over two chambers with valves. These have been superseded by more efficient multi-diaphragm units which are direct-driven and are more compact and reliable. These three and four chambered units have improved suction, less water pulsation and a more stable water flow.

The flexible impeller pump

These units normally have a pump with bronze casing and nitrile or neoprene impeller. The flexible rubber impeller allows operation in either direction. The direction of rotation will determine the suction and discharge ports of the pump.

The principal advantage of the flexible impeller pump is the ability to self prime. As the impeller rotates the rubber vanes flex and compress when they meet the cam area and expand when they pass the cam. This creates a suction vacuum that draws water or fluids into the pump. The water is then carried by the vanes around the pump chamber to the discharge port where it is forced out as the vanes compress again.

The pumped liquid provides lubrication. Failure to use liquid will generally ruin the impeller. These pumps do have long service lives compared to other pumps. They are self-priming and can be mounted clear of the bilge, with suction via a strainer. The maximum pressures are around 20psi.

The impeller either sucks up the water due to the flexing action of the impeller vanes against the contoured pump chamber walls or as the vanes spin past the pump ports. These pumps do have a more even and pulsation free water flow.

Pump impeller materials

Pump flexible-blade impellers come in a number of different compounds. Choose the correct type for optimum life and efficiency. Impeller types are as follows:

1. **Neoprene.** These are typically found in bronze pumps and are suitable for bilge pumping duties. Temperature range is 4°C to 80°C. Use at the outer temperature limits reduces performance and service life. They must not be used to pump oil-based fluids as the impeller can absorb oil compounds and expand. The result is that on the next start-up the binding impeller is destroyed. Always flush out a line if oily fluids are used.

2. **Nitrile.** These are designed for pumping fuel but they are also suited to pumping oil- and fuel-contaminated engine bilges. Temperature range is 10°C to 90°C. Use at the upper temperature limits reduces performance and service life. Nitrile impellers have a flow rate 30% lower than neoprene impellers so they should not be used in any high temperature applications.

Water pump impeller troubleshooting

If the pump impeller is damaged the following are possible causes:

1. If there are pieces missing out of the blade tips at the center of the impeller, pitting at the ends, or the edges have a hollowed out appearance, this is caused by cavitation. It is due to low pressures at the pump inlet and can be rectified by reducing inlet pipe restrictions and lengths, and increasing inlet pipe diameters.

2. If the impeller blade tips and end faces are worn, or the impeller drive is worn, this is also caused by cavitation, due to low pressures at the pump inlet, and the same measures apply.

3. If the end faces of the impeller have a hard and polished appearance, or there is some or all blades missing, this is caused by running the pump dry. The pump should not be run longer than 30 seconds with fluids, and stopped as soon as the fluids are gone.

4. If the impeller blades have excessive or permanent distortion or curving, this is caused by chemical action, excessive pump storage periods, or the end of the normal service life. Chemical effects result from pumping incorrect fluids.

5. If the impeller binds inside the pump housing, or the blades appear longer than the hub, or the impeller rubber is sticky and soft, this is caused by chemical actions, high fluid temperatures or long term immersion. Pumps should be flushed clean after use, and drained if being stored. High fluid temperatures should not be used.

6. If the impeller blades are 50% cracked or parts of the blade are missing, this is due to the impeller reaching the normal end of its operational life. It may also be the result of high output pressures, and fluids either high or low temperature. Running the pump dry can cause similar damage. Check and reduce pump pressures, or outlet pipe restrictions such as long pipe runs or blockages.

Impeller pump installation

As a vacuum is required the suction line and connections must be air tight to be efficient. A common problem is loose hoses and connections or hose clamps. Suction cannot form and it will not pump. This also causes impeller wear and damage, or shaft seal damage so pumps are not tolerant to running dry. The suction line diameter to an impeller pump should always be at least the same size as the impeller pump inlet port. Never make it smaller as the insufficient fluid will be available to the pump and this will cause impeller failure and cavitation.

Running the pump dry

The pumped liquid provides pump lubrication. In general you should never run a pump dry for more than 20 seconds. The friction of running dry will create significant heat and will burn and melt the impeller. It is always advisable to maintain suction lift to a maximum of 6 feet or much less.

Maintaining a vacuum

The same applies to engine water pumps. When replacing the cam or end cover always make sure that you coat the screw threads with something to seal it such as grease. Gaskets also must be absolutely free of damage and also complete cleanliness is required.

Pressure switches

The pressure switch is used to cut off and start the pump when pressure either falls to switch set value or exceeds the higher maximum value. Switches essentially have a small micro switch located inside the housing. The switch is activated by a spring-loaded plunger arrangement on the pump output housing. The most common cause of failure is a sticking switch or the rubber diaphragm seal.

The pressure switch is wired directly in line with the pump motor electrical positive wire. When the switch opens the power goes off, and when it closes the power goes on.

Water pump wiring

A couple of installation points must be observed when installing water pumps.

1. **Wire Sizes.** Ensure that the wire is rated for maximum current draw and voltage drop. Voltage drop problems are very common, and over sizing the wire is a good practice.

2. **Wire Connections.** Wire connections directly connected to the water pump are common, and you should ensure that the wire crimps are done properly. Also put some Vaseline over the connection to stop moisture getting into the connection lugs. Where wire tails require a butt splice, ensure that they are crimped properly. Some pumps with integral pressure switches require connection directly to one side so ensure this is properly done.

3. **Bonding.** Some metal cased pumps, such as wash down pumps should be bonded. This should be taken to the negative polarity of the supply. In the even of a positive short circuit to the case, this will ensure that the circuit breaker trips.

Why a water system strainer?

The water strainer is installed in the water suction line to the pump. Its primary purpose is to protect the pump from damaging sediment and particles from the storage tank. Observe the following:

1. **Element Cleaning.** It is essential to clean regularly the stainless steel strainer. Blockages are most frequent when commissioning a new vessel, or after refilling an empty tank. I have seen a number of vessels where the element has been removed because the owners were tired of cleaning blockages. The result will be early pump failure. Better to clean the system and eliminate the cause.

2. **Bowl Seals.** After cleaning the element, ensure that a good seal is made with the transparent inspection cover. Imperfect seals can cause air and contamination to be drawn into the system. Make sure that the seal is in good condition. A smear of Vaseline or silicon grease often helps.

What are water system accumulators?

The accumulator is an essential part of any water system. The basic principle is that air will compress under pressure and the water will not. The accumulator is a tank filled with air that fills to approximately 50% with water when the pump operates. After the pump stops running, the compressed air provides pressurized water stored within the accumulator.

It serves two functions, the first being a pressure buffer or cushion which absorbs fluctuations or spikes in pressure. This pulsation is an inherent characteristic of diaphragm pumps.

The effect is to operate quietly, and the pump pressure switch is able to reach the cut-off pressure, which increases the life of the pump, motor and the pressure switch. The life of the pump is extended, as the accumulator will prevent the pump operating as soon as the water outlet is opened. The larger the accumulator installed, the less often a pump is required to operate. When large demand systems are installed, larger accumulators are required.

Accumulator types

Accumulators are available in two main types:

1. **Non-pressurized.** These units are typically plastic cylinders, which are installed upright within the system. These also have a cock at the top to vent off air within the water system. With no bladders to separate the air and water, the tank must be drained every few months, as the air gradually disappears and the tank no longer functions as an accumulator. There must be air inside.

2. **Pressurized.** These accumulator types have an internal membrane or bladder that can be externally air pressurized with a bicycle pump, or factory pressurized with nitrogen. At installation the following procedure must be performed:

   1. Turn the pump off.

   2. Open the outlets and release the system pressure.

   3. Using a car tire pressure gauge, release nitrogen until pressure falls to 5 psi below pump cut-in pressure.

   4. If too much pressure is relieved, use a bicycle pump to increase to correct pressure.

Water filters

Filters should be fitted to all drinking water outlets. In most cases, this is the galley outlet. A filter will remove small particles, off tastes and smells caused by tank-water purification chemicals, as well as some bacteria. These form in pipes and tanks during extended periods of inactivity. You can sterilize the system.

Always install a filter with easily replaceable filter elements and replace promptly when stated service life is completed. The Whale types simply require a unit replacement, and Jabsco has the Aqua Filter. Always cleanse the water system before installing a new filter. Filters are generally manufactured of activated carbon. Filters that use porous ceramic, which removes all particles and detectable bacteria, will provide better water quality. A good filter should always come with a test report issued by an appropriate authority. It should be rated for the expected flow rate and should be renewed on the due date. A filter can never substitute for clean tanks. If you rely only on the filter, you risk the safety and health of all on board.

Shore water systems

Marina facilities have expanded and become more sophisticated worldwide. Many vessels are able to connect to electrical power, telephone, cable TV, Internet, water, and sewage. In many cases a permanent municipal shore water connection is made but this can pose some problems.

The normal shore water pressures are usually significantly higher than onboard system pressures. Where regulation units are installed, they filter the water, and then regulate down to onboard system pressure. The system can incorporate a solid state bilge sensor that will automatically close an inlet solenoid, and activate an alarm should the bilge water level rise, as well as activate the bilge pump. This is to ensure, that should there be a system leak, there is minimal flooding.

Figure 2-3 Shore Water Systems

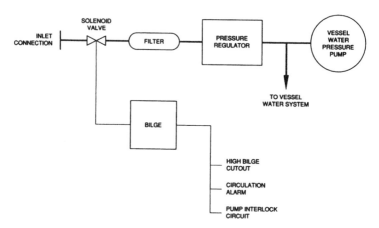

3. HOT WATER SYSTEMS

The calorifier or hot water system is becoming one of those hard-to-do-without luxuries. It is not difficult to install or incorporate into a system, and it even functions as an additional water reserve. The term calorifier is given as most marine hot water systems heat from inbuilt coils (calorific transfer) supplied from heated engine cooling water or on the old tramp ships I once served on, steam. It makes sense to utilize all the available energy consumed by the engines.

1. **Heating Coils.** The majority of units are fitted with a single copper heating coil. Beware of the cheaper imported units, as the coils are very small and have only a turn or two. Good calorifiers will have several turns installed to ensure good heat transfer rates.

2. **Electric Elements.** Calorifiers should also incorporate an auxiliary electric heating element for mains AC heating capability.

Element Ratings

Element ratings should not exceed 1200-1800 watts due to electrical supply limitations of shore power and small generators, unless you have a reasonably high output generator set.

Safety Thermostats

A thermostat is also essential for controlling temperature and preventing overheating and therefore over pressure conditions.

Pressure Relief Valves

All calorifiers should have a pressure relief valve. The valve should be regularly operated manually to ensure that it is not seized, and to clear away any insects or debris from the overflow pipe.

Inlet Valves

The inlet of a calorifier should always have a non-return (check) valve fitted to prevent the heated and expanding water in the tank from back flowing into the cold water system and pressurizing it.

Tank Insulation

Ensure that the calorifier has a good insulation layer or cover to avoid wastage of heat. If the engine is run every alternate day, good insulation will keep it warm over the extended period.

Tank Mounting

The calorifier must be mounted with the coil on the same level as, or below, the engine cooling water source. This is because the engine pump must circulate water through a longer system, which introduces resistance. This could bring to an overload of the pump.

Air Locks

There must be no air locks in the system as these also go through the engine cooling system and affect cooling. The calorifier must always be installed lower than the engine water filling point.

Hose Connections

Use heat resistant rubber hoses to connect up heating circuit. Ensure that air locks cannot form in the hoses. Ensure that all hose connections have double hose clamps.

Figure 3-1 Calorifier

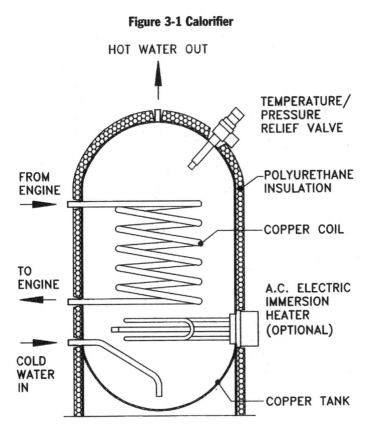

Diesel hot water heaters

The compact diesel hot water system is now becoming common-place on vessels. This unit can also be part of a central heating system. Companies such as Eberspacher, Mikuni, Webasto and Hurricane have very efficient systems. The Webasto is illustrated below.

Figure 3-2 Diesel Hotwater System

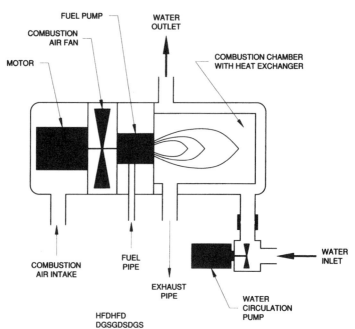

HFDHFD
DGSGDSDGS

Diesel water heater operation

The typical operational cycle is as follows:

a. **Starting.** An electric fan draws in cold air to the heat exchanger/burner. This is normally from the engine area.

b. **Ignition.** Fuel is drawn in at the same time by the fuel pump from the main tank and mixed with the air. Ignition takes place in a combustion chamber and the fuel is ignited by an electric glowplug.

c. **Combustion.** The combustion takes place within a sealed exchanger and the exhaust gases are expelled to atmosphere.

d. **Heating.** An integrated water pump circulates the water through the heat exchanger and subsequently to the calorifier and heating radiators. A thermostat in the cabin shuts the system down and operates to maintain set temperature. Eberspacher has developed an automatic quarter heat control to reduce unnecessary cycling, which improves the fuel economy.

Water system troubleshooting

The Pump Will Not Prime (No Discharge)

1. Restricted inlet or blockage in pipe. Check and clear any blockages

2. Restricted outlet. Check for any restrictions and clear

3. Air leak in suction or discharge line. Check all joints and clamp points

4. Pump diaphragm ruptured. The pump will require dismantling to check

5. Debris under flapper valves. The pump will require dismantling to check

6. Pump housing fractured. Check housing for cracks

7. Strainer clogged. This is common; remove, clean, and ensure strainer housing seals properly

8. Valve closed. Make sure all valves are open

9. Kink in water pipe or hose. Check all bends and remove kinks

10. No water in tank. Check your water tank levels

11. Clogged one-way valve. Remove, clean and check that flapper valve operates

12. Discharge head too high. Check the system

13. Low battery voltage (pump is running slow). Check electrical connections; a bad connection will cause high resistance and voltage drop

14. Pump seized, or debris in same. Check pump section for debris and clean

The Water Pump Will Not Operate

1. Circuit breaker tripped or fuse failed. Reset and replace fuses. If it blows instantaneously this means short circuit was due to seized pump. Slow to trip indicates pump bearing or perhaps poor connections cause the problem

2. Pump connection loose or broken. Check all electrical connections

3. Pressure switch fault. Check the switch, bypass it. It may require replacement.

4. Motor fault. A seized motor will generally trip breaker

5. Pump seized, or debris in same. Check and clean. Try and rotate pump manually

6. Wiring/connection failure. Check electrical connections and repair as required

7. Restricted pump delivery, filter blockage. Check and clean

The Water Flow Is Pulsating

1. Accumulator. The bellows type may require adjustment

2. Suction hose or pipe too small. Renew the suction piping

3. System or pipe pressure leak. Check all parts of the systems

4. Water outlet leaking. Check all parts of the systems

The Pump Cycles On and Off Excessively

1. Accumulator problem. The bellows type may require adjustment

2. Water tank empty. When near empty the pump starts to lose suction

3. Pump diaphragm ruptured. Open and check the pump

4. Discharge line/pipes leaking. Check all parts of the systems, check tighten hose clamp joints

The Pump Will Not Switch Off

1. Pressure switch fault. The pump will not reach cut-off pressure. Check pressure switch and replace as required

2. Debris under valves. Check the pump and clean

3. Air leak on pump inlet hose. Check hose clamp joints and tighten

4. Strainer clogged. This is common. Open and clean the strainer

5. Pump diaphragm, or impeller or valves worn. Open and check the condition

6. Pump diaphragm ruptured. Open and check the condition

Water system maintenance

Winterizing. For those in colder climates, proper winterization is essential to prevent freezing and damage. Perform the following protective measures:

1. **Remove Pump.** If possible, remove the entire pump and store it in a dry place.

2. **Drain System.** The most practical precaution is to totally drain the water system, including the pump and accumulator. Do not use anti-freeze solutions in the potable water system.

Maintenance

Opening the faucets or outlet and depressurization of the system when the power is turned off can increase the life of the pump. This reduces unnecessary wear on pump diaphragms and valves.

4. GALLEY PLUMBING SYSTEMS

Even the smallest boats have self-draining sinks and either on-demand cold or even hot water, or a manually pumped freshwater faucet.

Galley Drain

The galley drain is usually a simple reinforced hose that connects the sink drain to a seacock located below the static waterline of the boat. On yachts where the sink will not drain on one tack this creates a problem. Another potential problem is that the same sink drain can cause seawater to flood in when the seacock is left open. When designing or refitting a galley the drain should be put in above the normal heeled waterline to avoid this situation. Another option is to install a two-way valve in the drain line with the extra line running to a pump. The pump can be a small manual diaphragm bilge pump that discharges above the waterline. It is sometimes installed through the transom area.

P-Traps

In your home all sinks incorporate a double loop such as a P-trap located below the drain. This creates a pool of water to seal the drain opening from odors coming from the sewage system. This isn't always so effective on a boat when it is heeling. P-traps are useful for catching things that accidentally could go down the sink such as your rings. Straight through hoses tend to be cleaner to maintain.

The galley sink

Galley sinks generally vary with the size of the galley. Ideally it is always good to have a sink with an integral draining board. Also the question of a single or a double one arises. The deeper than normal sink is useful for keeping an accumulation of dishes when washing conditions are not ideal at sea. Also sinks should have the fill-in board or integral chopping board option to maximize bench and work space. I have personally always opted for one deep and as large as possible sink that allows everything from dishes to clothes washing. If you are lucky you can find one with a single draining board as well. While the deeper sinks do have drainage problem this can be resolved. Size compatibility with the plug hole fittings and the pipe work can be a problem.

Manual galley pumps

While most boats have pressurized on-demand water systems serving both galley and shower or a switched pump, the option of a backup manual pump is sensible. Many galleys have a manual or a small electrically-operated salt water supply to the galley sink. This obviously saves valuable fresh water for washing dishes.

This is often sourced from the engine cooling water system to avoid a separate seacock. The most common type is the piston type lift pumps that incorporate their own faucet. They are not generally rated for seawater so they have a limited life. Also common are manual foot pumps to serve the same function. Those from Whale have double action and very efficient.

5. WATERMAKER SYSTEMS

Water resources are always limited on board, and this affects the maximum cruising ranges of most boats. The most practical system is the reverse-osmosis desalinator, although evaporative systems are economical for long-term engine use in ocean-going motor and trawler yachts.

You should never make water within 10 miles of a coastline. Many coastal waters are often polluted to levels well above World Health Organization (WHO) recommendations and this can be carried into the tanks with product water.

Reverse osmosis principles

When a semi-permeable membrane separates fresh and salt water, the natural osmosis is for the fresh water to flow through to the salt-water side. To reverse this process, salt water is pressurized to force the fresh water through the membrane out of the salt water. Seawater is pressurized by a priming pump and filtered to remove particles. Then the high-pressure pump increases pressure. The high-pressure water is then forced through the membranes. The membranes are housed in a high-pressure casing. The illustration below shows the basic principles of operation.

Figure 5-1 Reverse Osmosis Process

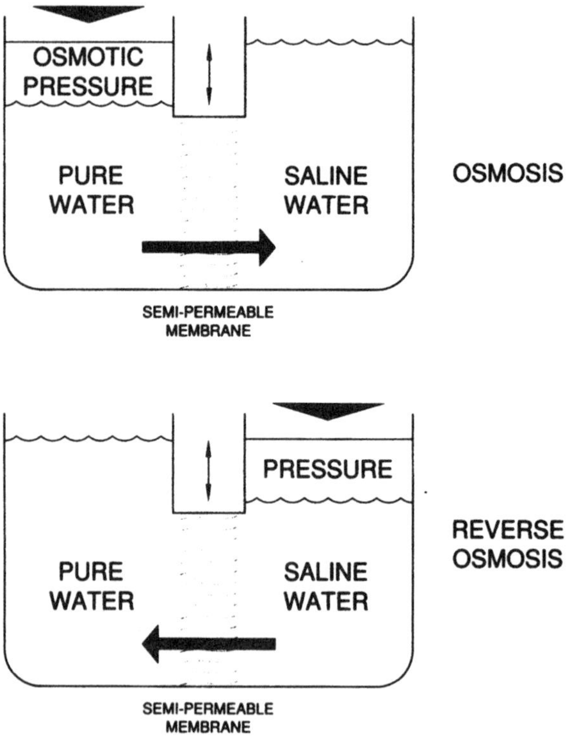

OSMOTIC PRESSURE

PURE WATER   SALINE WATER   OSMOSIS

SEMI-PERMEABLE MEMBRANE

PRESSURE

PURE WATER   SALINE WATER   REVERSE OSMOSIS

SEMI-PERMEABLE MEMBRANE

Monitoring and control

The Sea Recovery system is a typical system:

1. Raw seawater is supplied through the seawater inlet valve and sea strainer to the booster pump suction.

2. The seawater is then pressurized to 20 psi by the booster pump and supplied to the media filter. The 5 micron pre-filter and oil water filter remove sediments, suspended solids, silt and oil are removed. This water is pressure monitored with a gauge and low pressure switch, which stops the system when low pressure is detected.

3. The water is pressurized to around 900 psi by the high-pressure pump and regulated by a valve. This is also monitored and controlled by a high pressure switch.

4. The pressurized water enters the reverse osmosis membranes, which forces out the salt and minerals. A salinity probe monitors the product water quality, which also adjusts for the water temperature. The brine flows through a monitor and then is dumped through a discharge valve.

5. The product water is monitored, passed through a charcoal filter and UV sterilizer and is then sent to the potable water tanks.

6. The system also has an automatic fresh water flushing system, which flushes the system to reduce membrane fouling.

Figure 5-2 SeaFresh Desalination System

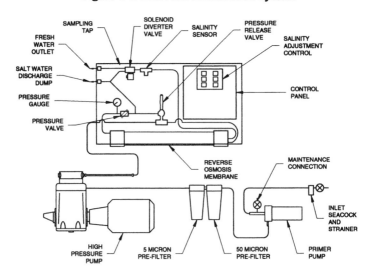

Watermaker membranes

Space and weight are always critical considerations. Many systems such as Sea Recovery, Spectra, SeaFresh and Pur have constantly tried to solve this problem. Many units have been reduced in both size and weight by the use of new membrane designs and low weight materials. Membranes are primarily manufactured from Thin Film Composite (TFC) and come in four types: spiral wound, flat layered, hollow fine line and tubular construction. Spiral wound is the most popular as it is easy to obtain. A membrane has an average life span of 3–5 years, entirely based on the input water quality, and the effectiveness of water pre-filtering. The typical output water quality of many small desalinators is around 300 ppm, which is virtually undetectable by even the most delicate taste buds.

While the overall size has not been reduced significantly the efficiency has improved. Pumps have improved efficiency and developments in the use of lower pump pressures resulted in reduced pump sizes. The use of slower revving pumps has also reduced both noise and vibration.

While membrane pressure cylinders have usually been made from stainless steel, many are now made from carbon fiber with stainless steel end plugs.

Membrane Cleaning

Membrane fouling, caused by organic molecules, suspended solids, bacteria and algae, as well as minerals, is a common problem. Pre-filters take out only some of the material. Cleaning is time consuming and requires the use of chemicals. A membrane should be used daily and if not, it requires preservation. Some manufacturers recommend freshwater flushing if the unit is to be idle for more than 10 days. In some units this is an automatic function. Failure to properly flush and preserve will result in very early destruction of the membranes. If your unit is flushed or filled with a biocide allow the water produced for the first 30 minutes to be dumped.

System monitoring and control

System monitoring varies from simple light indication and gauges to a sophisticated fully automated electronic control. Systems monitor for pump water pressure, salinity, filter and sea strainer condition, self diagnostics, pressure warnings, running hours, water output volumes and more. Some units also control and monitor ultraviolet sterilizer units. Many units now incorporate automatic pressure regulation to the membranes.

Powering the high pressure pump

Many pumps can be run directly off the engine. This is a good option if it can be set up. The pump load will be useful and help reduce the damaging light loading conditions associated with battery charging runs. The pumps tend to have 2–3 belts so some engineering will be required. Pumps are also available in 12 volts DC, 24 volts DC and 120-230 volts AC. DC pumps have a significant current draw so running the engine and providing the electrical load from the alternator is best. The smaller 35 liters per hour models can use only 100 watts (8 amps).

Watermaker installation

Through-hull fittings are required for raw seawater intake and the overboard brine discharge. Do not take the seawater input from auxiliary engine or generator water inlets as this will starve the system of water.

Install a y-valve on the input to the watermaker. One is to salt water and one is from the fresh water tank. The freshwater line should have a check valve and an isolation valve. This will allow easy fresh water flushing.

Outputs and membrane correction factors

In a good desalination system, the salt rejection rates are typically 99% in the ph ranges 4 to 11 at operating pressure range of 700–900 psi. In these conditions the output is unaffected by pressure and temperature. Where temperatures and pressures change correction factors must be applied to ensure improved production rates.

Figure 5-3 Desalinator Temperature Correction Factors

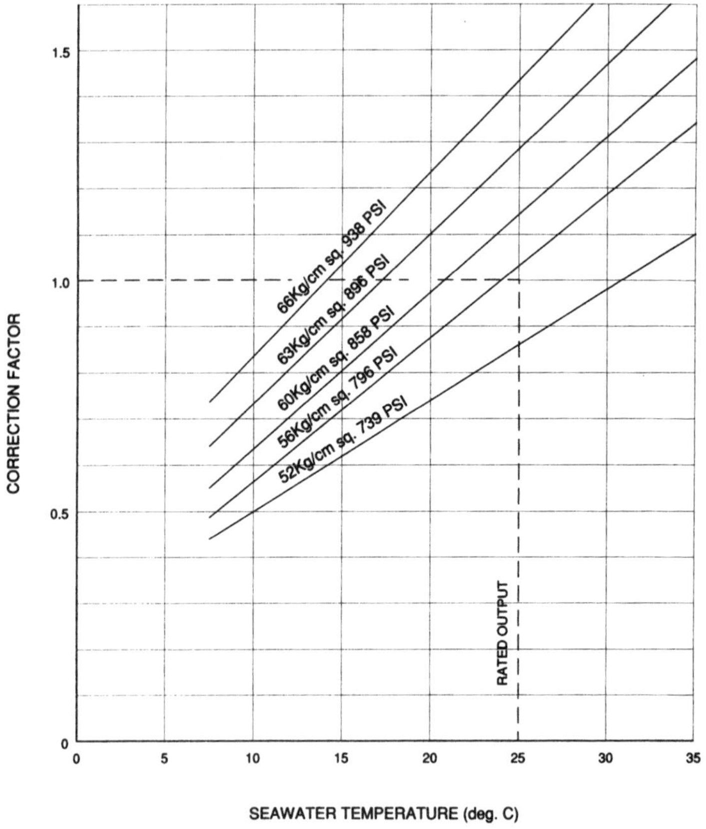

Watermaker maintenance

These are typical maintenance procedures that will vary depending on manufacturers and models.

1. Clean inlet strainer at the same time as the engine strainer.

2. Pre-filters can be washed 5 or 6 times before replacement. This equals approximately 80 hours operation in clean waters.

3. Disinfect membranes to prevent biological fouling for shutdown periods exceeding 10–14 days using recommended biocides. Failure to do this will significantly reduce output and damage membranes. Never allow membranes to dry out.

4. Check pressure pump oil levels and renew every 500 hours.

5. Check and re-tension rubber drive belts every 6 months.

6. Clean membranes when output drops below 15% of rated output or when product salinity increases. This occurs through the build-up of grime, biological material and mineral scale. Do not open the pressure vessel to do this. Cleaning should be done according to the manufacturer's recommendations. This usually entails the use of alkaline and detergent cleaners to remove organic material, and acidic cleaners to remove mineral scale.

Desalinator troubleshooting

Low Water Flow

1. The seawater inlet strainer may be blocked. Open and clean out all debris

2. The seawater pre-filter may be blocked. Clean or replace the filter element

3. The membranes may be fouled. Clean membranes using recommended procedure

4. The seawater pump belts if fitted may be loose and slipping. Re-tension the belts

No Product Water Flow

1. The seawater pump has stopped. The circuit breaker may have tripped. Check the circuit breaker and reset and if it trips start troubleshooting the circuit. Overload of pump or short circuit in connection box wiring are the usual reasons

2. Check the pump drive belts if fitted, and renew or re-tension as required

3. The electromagnetic clutch is not operating. This can be due to broken wiring connection or the clutch coil has failed

Circuit Breaker Tripping

1. The pump clutch coil has failed. The clutch wire can be grounding out

2. The water pump is seizing. This will require overhaul and possible replacement. Pump bearing failure is also a possible cause

Low Working Pressure

1. The overpressure relief valve is leaking. Check the valve. It may require overhaul, replacement or recalibration

2. Water pump fault. If the pump does not have the correct output pressure, production will be incorrect

3. The brine dump valve jammed open. Verify that the valve is closing properly. Brine crystal growth under the solenoid valve can occur

Product Water Salty

1. The membranes may be fouled. Clean membranes using recommended procedure

2. Excess working pressure. Reduce the working pressure

6. SALT WATER SYSTEMS

Salt water is often used for washdown pumps, and also for the galley, toilet flushing and Livewell applications on fishing boats.

A through hull skin fitting and a seacock with the hoses make up the system. Both should be of the highest standard.

Washdown pumps have many uses, for washing decks down, rinsing off the blood and scales when fishing, cooling yourself down on a hot day, cleaning anchor rodes and a lot more. Wash down pump units can be completely integrated with pressure switches, filters etc. Typically they deliver 5–10 gallons a minute and draw around 6–10 amps.

Bait Livewell timers

Keeping live bait alive in a tank requires clean oxygenated water. Livewell pumps generally have a timer installed in the circuit to the pump. The timer will automatically switch the pump on and off. Some have variable settings. A typical time setting is 30 seconds of operation every three to five minutes. This will keep your bait fish alive without drawing too much battery power. Many systems also allow continuous operation as well.

7. BILGE PUMP SYSTEMS

Bilge pumps play a crucial safety role in any vessel. The tendency is simply to get the cheapest unit available and install it. Manual and electrical bilge pumps should be of the highest quality, installed correctly and maintained. The following factors should be considered when selecting and installing bilge pumps. There are basically two types, the submersible centrifugal pump and the diaphragm pump. Submersible pumps cannot be maintained or repaired.

Pump head pressure

Head pressure is related to the height that the water must be lifted to. All pumps have maximum head figures for a particular model. The higher the head the lower the flow rate; in submersible pumps the flow rate drops off very quickly. Most pumps are rated at zero head, so for any pump you should reduce the actual flow rate by around 5% for every foot of head pressure. In most boats that will be 15–20% on an average installation.

Bilge pump flow rates

Most bilge pumps are listed with flow rates, which are designated as liters or gallons per hour or minute. Many recommend using a pump with a minimum capacity of 1000 gallons per hour. Flow rates should be noted with caution as they are often quoted at an open flow rate, and in a boat installation the head they have to pump lowers that rating. Always look at the pump specification to see what the rating is against, usually it is at 12 volts and zero head. In some cases the flow rate may be quoted at 13.6 volts, with engine alternator supplying power. This can drop at normal battery level by anything from 5 to 30%.

Submersible bilge pumps

The centrifugal pump is the most common in use. It is important to always buy and install the very best quality you can. Cheaper pumps are very unreliable, and tend not to last long. Pumps have the following general characteristics:

1. **Motor Rating.** Motors should be rated continuously. Some are not, so make a check. The pump motors are also cooled by the bilge water they pump. One model I had recently was not recommended for anything but standing water, and it could not cope with serious water ingress. It failed within 9 months.

2. **Motor Type.** Motors generally use a permanent magnet motor, which means no brushes.

3. **Dry Running.** Dry running does not damage the pump impellers, though motors require water to cool them.

4. **Automatic Bilge Pumps.** There are pumps that have an integral "computer chip" that cycles the pump on every 2–3 minutes. The pump then stops if no water is detected. Some units will only switch on when water is detected.

Diaphragm bilge pumps

They are self-priming and can be mounted clear of the bilge, with the suction line having a strainer in line at the suction source. They can be operated dry without damage, and so tend to suit many typical shallow sailing yacht and power boat bilges.

Automatic bilge control systems

Automation of bilge pumps is very common. There are a number of important considerations to consider when putting in any automated control:

1. **Pollution.** There are very heavy fines for the wilful or accidental discharge of oily wastes into harbors and coastal waters. It is the environmental responsibility of all boat owners not to discharge any waste into the sea. Any bilge that can have oil in it must never be fitted with an automatic pumping system.

2. **Controls.** Automatic switches are notoriously unreliable. If the float or device stays on the bilge pump may burn out and probably ruin a set of batteries by totally flattening them.

Automatic bilge control

Float or level switching devices are now available and may use a number of different technical operational principles.

Mechanical Float. This is by far the most common device and probably the most reliable if the float switch is of high quality, if the bilge is free of debris or cannot be fouled by the pump cable. The mechanical float incorporates either mercury, which is being phased out, or a metal ball bearing that bridges out the pump activation contacts. Some units use a magnet to activate a reed switch.

Figure 7-1 Bilge Control Schematics

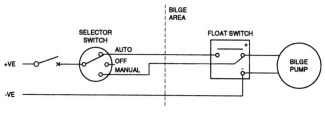

STANDARD BILGE CONTROL

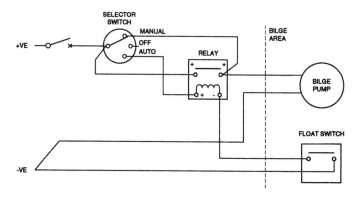

Solid-state Devices. These include the ultrasonic, conductive probes and capacitive types. While some appear to work well, there are a great number of failures. Some cheaper units can cause electrolytic corrosion problems. If the probes are fouled or coated with oil they often don't work. One advantage of some is a delay feature that requires continued water presence over 15–20 seconds to activate which prevents pump from start and stop cycling in rough water conditions.

Optical Devices. These devices resolve many of the problems normally encountered with units using probes. They operate on a rather innovative principle. The pump units are controlled by an optical fluid switch. The unit emits a light pulse every 30 seconds. If the lens is immersed in water, the light beam refracts. The change in direction of the beam is sensed by a coating inside the lens, and triggers the pump control circuit. The units also have time delay circuits that can be adjusted for periods of 20–140 seconds so that the pump will drain the bilge after water clears the sensor.

Air Devices. These are relatively old but simple devices, which are very reliable. They depend on the pressure of water in a tube to activate a switch via a diaphragm.

Ultrasonic Devices. These are not that reliable and I would suggest using more proven systems.

Bilge alarms

A bilge alarm is a very good safety system to install. In many cases you can be unaware that a bilge pump is switched on and running continuously. In some cases the pump is unable to keep up with the water ingress and the first time you know you have a problem is when you observe the water down below. When a boat is running under engine, you might also not hear an alarm so any system should incorporate both visual and audible functions.

The best method is simply installing a float switch, wired to a relay that will activate a light and the audible alarm device.

Figure 7-2 Bilge Alarm Circuit

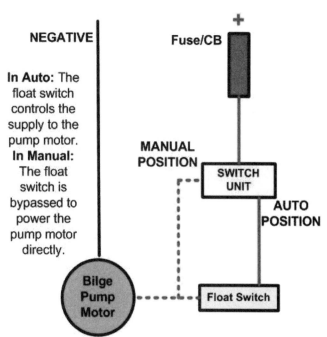

Manual bilge pumps

It is normal to have one manual or hand operated diaphragm pump that can be operated from the cockpit or deck. Manual bilge pumps are usually large bore units with a single diaphragm. It is important to choose a unit that can be operated for significant periods and location is a consideration.

These lever-operated pumps are designed to produce a good water flow rate against a relatively low head. At high heads the actual effort required to work them becomes excessive. The pumps are typically self-priming to several meters and may be either single acting or double acting.

The double acting pump is in effect two pumps that are connected using a common activation lever. They produce water flow on both the forward and backward stroke of the same handle. In any boat the greater the efficiency the better.

Typically they are constructed of die-cast, epoxy coated and anodized alloys. They use a synthetic neoprene rubber or nitrile diaphragm. The flow rates vary; nominal is around 10 to 35 gallons per minute at a rate of 70 strokes per minute. Always carry a spare diaphragm kit on board.

Centrifugal pumps

Centrifugal pumps are often required under survey rules. They give a smooth and high output at low pressure. The actual flow rates will depend on water inlet restrictions and discharge as well the head heights.

These pumps use a spinning impeller with a centrifugal force to move the water. The level of the water that is being pumped must be at a height above the pump sufficient for gravity to force the water into the pump. If it is not the pump will require priming with water.

They are not cheap to install but they pump huge volumes, will pass some bilge debris and will also double as deck wash pumps and help with fire fighting.

They can be belt driven from your engine and are available with either manual or electromagnetic clutch for remote control. The circuit is similar to a refrigeration electric clutch circuit. After use, the supply must be switched off to avoid burning out the coil.

Installing two bilge pumps

The choice of the right bilge pump is often one of compromise. You need to install a pump large enough to handle an emergency and small enough to maintain dry bilges and pump small volumes of water. The ideal setup is a relatively small bilge pump with a flow rate of around 400 gph, connected with a float switch to give automatic operation. The small bilge pump handles the minor rainwater and shaft-gland water leakage. The second bilge pump should be a very high capacity pump of around 3,500 gph, mounted a little higher, usually 2–3 inches, in the bilge to handle serious and boat threatening water ingress.

The smaller pump will require a ½- or ¾-inch hose and the large pump 1 or even 1½-inch depending on your choice. It is a matter of preference. I have the main large pump set on a manual operation arrangement. In addition I would recommend a bilge alarm wired up to a float switch set at the main bilge pump height. If the alarm sounds you know you have a problem and need to switch the pump on.

Bilge Pump Electrical Connections

There are some important factors to ensure the reliability of electric bilge pumps.

1. If the cable is long enough, make connections above maximum bilge water levels. Good bilge pumps use tinned copper wiring.

2. Ensure that any automatic float switch is rated for the maximum pump current. Otherwise serious voltage drops could cause pump problems.

3. The supply to the automatic float switch arrangement must be taken from the supply side to the main power isolation switch if the pump is to remain in automatic operation when the power is switched off. Always double check this function.

4. As a minimum use crimp butt splices to make wiring connections. Consider soldering each connection and covering the joint with heat shrink insulation. The overall cable should also be covered in heat shrink or wrapped in self-amalgamating tape. This will generally prevent the joint interacting with salt water and failing. Always make sure that connections are kept separate so that any short circuit between them is impossible.

5. The ABYC and normal electrical protection practice require that a circuit be fused or has a circuit breaker rated for the cable size, typically 15 amps. Always oversize the bilge pump wiring sizes. At maximum output rating I would suggest to aim for 3% maximum voltage drop. Many disagree with this based on a nuisance trip of a circuit breaker or blowing of the fuse, stopping the pump and allowing flooding to occur or worse. Many prefer not to protect the circuit for this reason. Faults that would trip a breaker or blow a fuse are faults within the wiring connections, or the pump is jammed and the motor stalls with an overload condition. It is rare that a pump motor short circuits internally. The answer is to install a larger than required cable and protect that cable, which will give a significant margin for overloads and also slight overloads caused by temporary jamming of impellers or tight pump bearings. If you have a major fault the breaker will trip eventually before overheating of the wiring occurs, creating a fire risk. Do not use fuses for protection as they are relatively unreliable.

How much current does the pump draw?

Pump flow rate (gph)	Average current in amps at 12 volts
400	2 amps
800	2.8 amps
1000	3.3 amps
1500	4.8 amps
2000	8.4 amps
3700	15.5 amps

Installing a bilge pump

Do you know that more boats sink alongside the dock than at sea? It is true and it's often due to bilge pump deficiencies. Many people buy and then badly install undersized low quality pumps. Bilge pumps must be properly installed if they are to operate correctly and reliably.

1. Always mount the pump or the suction in the lowest part of bilge and keep this a short distance from the bottom to avoid drawing in bilge sediments. Automatic float switches should be positioned to cut out the pump at the selected water level.

2. Never place the pump in the bilge without securing it. This is a very common mistake. If the pump falls over, it will not suction water properly and draw air possibly burning out the pump. Bilge pump brackets are supplied that should be secured to a stringer or alternatively some bolts can be fastened using epoxy into the bottom of the bilge to mount the pump on. Always secure the automatic float switch to the bottom on the bilge well.

3. Always install a strainer on the suction side of centrifugal pumps. Submersible pumps have a strainer as an integral part of the base but these are rather coarse. It is quite common for bilge debris to jam the impeller. Some install a finer gauge wire cage over the pump to prevent this.

4. Always install smooth bore flexible discharge hoses. Corrugated hoses can reduce the pump output by up to 30%. Install smooth internal bore reinforced hoses as this will keep flow losses to a minimum. Use hoses that will not kink. Many pumps are ineffective due to kinks or constriction of the discharge line. Keep discharge hoses as short as practicable.

5. The discharge line must have a minimum of bends and long runs as this will reduce the pump output. Keep the output hose as short and straight as practicable. This will mean considering the discharge location carefully, either local hull or transom.

6. The overboard discharge must be above the waterline. There is a trend to install at water level to reduce splash and hull staining, but this is inherently dangerous. If the pump discharge is submerged when the pump is running, the water may siphon back through the pump into the bilge when the pump stops, flooding and even sinking your boat. In auto mode the float switch may start and pump out and keep cycling on and off eventually draining the batteries. The discharge should always be above the deepest heel angle or with transom installations above the level at maximum squat.

7. Always use a vented anti-siphon loop on the overboard discharge line to prevent any back siphoning.

8. Use a thin-wall through-hull fitting on the overboard discharge. Many pump discharges are restricted as thick-wall fittings are used.

9. Always use two hose clamps on every hose connection as a safety precaution.

Bilge pump maintenance

Regular maintenance is essential.

1. Regularly clean bilges of sediment and debris that can clog filters and pumps.

2. Operate pumps on a monthly basis with some water in the bilges. Many bilge pumps are found to be seized after months or even years of non-operation. Some submersible pumps have the impeller attached with a screw. The low grade stainless on my pump corroded off, the impeller came off and the motor shaft was spinning in the impeller boss. The boat nearly sank.

Bilge pump troubleshooting

The Water Flow Rate Is Low

1. The most probable fault is that the strainer is blocked with debris. Open and clean out and try again

2. The pump impeller is fouled. This is also a common fault. Clean out and try again

3. The suction hose is kinked. Take the kink out, often this happens because the hose has a sharp bend

4. The suction hose is blocked with debris. You will need to remove and clean the hose

5. The suction line has an air lock. Look for air leaks in the suction side

6. Low battery voltage

The Water Pump Will Not Operate

1. The circuit breaker has tripped. Check that pump isn't seized or water and corrosion in connections

2. The float switch is fouled (usually with debris). This is a common fault

3. The float switch connections are corroded and connections should not be immersed

The Pump Will Not Switch Off

1. The float switch is fouled (usually with debris). This is a common fault. Also check that the wires to the float switch are not fouling and holding the float

2. The float switch is mounted too low. Check whether the actually level is correct

3. The float switch has a wire connection short circuit. This is common where connections are immersed

The Circuit Breaker Is Tripping

1. The pump impeller or motor may be seized. Check that the impeller is not jammed with debris

2. The float switch has a wire connection short circuit. This is common where connections are immersed

3. The pump motor windings may be short circuited. This will require a new pump.

8. SHOWER (GRAY) WATER SYSTEMS

Shower sumps, sump pumps and their related control systems are often cause for problems. Shower waste water is commonly known as gray water. The majority of sail and power boats have pre-manufactured plastic water collection sumps installed. These units incorporate a small centrifugal submersible bilge pump along with a float switch to automatically operate the pump when the gray water level rises and falls. The shower base drains the water directly to the small sump, and it is pumped directly overboard by the pump. If you live in a zero discharge area, the pump or water outputs to a gray water holding tank and drain pump. The shower drain system generally requires specific pumps; commonly these are the same as bilge applications. The common pumps in use are as follows:

Diaphragm shower pumps

Jabsco and Whale have a range of purpose designed shower diaphragm pumps that eliminate the need for a sump pump and float switch. The pumps are self-priming, have four chambers, are connected directly to the drain outlet and have a strainer installed in-line on the suction side. These pumps have power consumption rates of around of 5–8 amps at full load. The Whale Gulper 220 pump is very reliable and effective. I have installed these on my own boat. They can be run dry; strainers are recommended to stop pump blockages.

Figure 8-1 Shower System

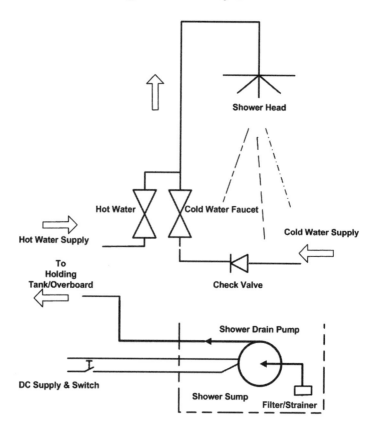

Submersible drain pumps

These plastic bilge pump types are common. Rule and others manufacture fully integrated sump, suction filter, pump and float switch units. The sump pump units usually have a check valve to prevent back siphoning and a clear cover for inspection.

Shower drain piping

The same principles apply with respect to using reinforced hoses. You should always install a siphon break in shower system overboard discharge lines. This also applies to galley gray water overboard drain lines. This will prevent inside flooding of the boat when the boat is heeled over.

Shower pump maintenance

Shower and sink drain pumps are prone to rapid filter clogging due to hair, soap residues and other debris. In automatic float switch units, hair and solidified soap often cause the float to stick. The filters should be checked and cleaned weekly, and the system flushed with hot water to dissolve residues.

Sump pump control

The float switch is frequently the most annoying part of shower sump systems. The mechanical float switch is the most common device in use, both for bilge and shower pump control. These float switches have an integral mercury, or more recently a mercury free switch located inside the float mechanism. It is important to make sure that the float switch wires are routed outside the sump enclosure. This reduces the chances of the wiring fouling the float, causing the pump not to start or continue running.

Installing a pump and float switch

When installing a pump it is common practice to fasten the strainer base and clip the pump into it. On my own boat I have installed a removable plate that fits the sump base. On this the strainer and the float switch are fastened. This allows the entire assembly to be easily removed for maintenance. A common problem is keeping the wiring and terminations away from the water. It is best to fasten these to the pump discharge piping to keep it neat. Allow a small loop in the wiring at the float switch so that the wiring does not stress or prevent the float from moving freely. Always slope the sump to one end and mount the pump at the lower end to allow the maximum volume of water to be pumped out, as some soapy water will always remain and this can smell.

Selecting a control system

To select manual or automatic control you will need a simple bilge pump panel with the Hand-Off-Auto setting. Quality waterproof switches and panels are available. The usual location for a panel is close to the shower but you should keep it well clear of shower water. Another useful option is to have a panel with an indicator light to show that the pump is running. You can usually hear a diaphragm pump operating. A centrifugal pump is very quiet, and if the float switch jams or you inadvertently leave the pump in manual, you can end up with the batteries drained down. Longer wiring runs to the switch unit can cause voltage drops; always increase the wiring size to compensate. A relay can be used but this can complicate the circuit unnecessarily.

9. SEWAGE (BLACK) WATER SYSTEMS

As most boaters know, the requirement for MSDs is changing around the world. In addition all boaters have a moral responsibility to dispose of sewage in an environmentally responsible method. In the US the Clean Vessel Act of 1992 is the primary legislation. In many countries, similar legislation is being introduced. The USCG requires all boats with a toilet to have some method of storing or treating the waste. It is important to comply with laws pertaining to illegal discharges. An MSD is any equipment for installation on board the vessel that is designed to receive, retain, treat or discharge sewage, and any process to treat the sewage. Boaters should make sure they understand the requirements. In some cases an overboard Y valve is prohibited so do check your local laws.

Human pathogenic enteric viruses in sea water or fresh water pose a potential risk to health through contact and consumption. The waters and shell fish have been contaminated by human fecal wastes. Infected humans, regardless of the presence of symptoms, can excrete millions of virus particles per gram of feces. Infectious virus particles can survive for several months in water under suitable environmental conditions. This cannot be assumed in every case as disease causing microbes such as Giardia, Hepatitis A virus, Cryptosporidium and Gastroenteritis causing viruses from human and animal feces, have now polluted our waters. Because there are millions of micro-organisms in a gram of feces, it only needs a tiny amount in water to cause pollution.

Discharge categories

There are three categories of discharge zones and there are three corresponding types of MSD defined by the USCG under the US Federal Pollution Control Act.

1. Three miles offshore, where you can discharge raw sewage waste directly overboard.

2. Less than three miles offshore, discharge of raw untreated sewage is prohibited. Waste must be sanitized by an on-board treatment system or held on board within a holding tank and discharged at an authorized station.

3. Zero Discharge. There are many areas that are designated zero discharge of any overboard waste, and you need to check whether you are in one. These areas include non-navigable inland lakes, and the Great Lakes.

What is a type I MSD?

This device uses chemicals to disinfect sewage. The discharge must be free of visible solids and meet standards for bacterial content. The sewage must be macerated to break up solids. The fecal coliform bacteria output must be at least 1000 colonies per 100 milliliters or less with no visible floating solids. These types macerate or chop up the waste to break up solids. There are 3 main manufacturers of Type 1 systems.

The Raritan LectraSan series of system operate using both salinity and electric current that consists of electrodes to break down the seawater to form chlorine (hypochlorous acid), a chlorinating agent that kills bacteria and disinfect the sewage. After treatment, the acid recombines to reform as salt water. The system requires 2 by 2 minute flushing cycles to transport the waste through the two waste treatment phases and overboard. This has a heavy electrical requirement of up 50 amps that must be factored into electrical load calculations.

The Raritan PuraSan MSD uses a solid tablet made of chlorine that produces a halogen solution to treat the waste. The halogen disinfectant is actually quite corrosive and you need to be aware of its impact on aluminum, copper and steel. In addition you need to be careful when handling chemicals. The electrical load is 10 amps for 2 by 2 minute flush cycles.

The SeaLand SanX system can be used in all waters but installation requirements are considerably more than the others and may suit larger vessels only. The SanX injects a chemical disinfectant agent into the treatment tank to mix with the macerated waste. The electrical load requirements are similar to the PuraSan unit.

The Groco Thermo-Pure system uses heat as the disinfection technique. Heat raises the waste temperature to a level that will kill bacteria. It requires substantial electrical power from a generator.

Note that Type 1 MSDs cannot discharge into No-Discharge zones.

What is a Type II MSD?

This is a device similar to Type I devices with a higher level of treatment and higher quality discharge. The fecal coliform bacteria output must be at least 200 colonies per 100 milliliters, with suspended solids of less than 150 milligrams per liter of discharge. The best-known devices are those from Microfors and Galleymaid. Cost and installation are considerably greater than Type I devices and are only for larger vessels.

What is a Type III MSD?

These systems use a holding tank to retain all waste on board. These MSDs have a USCG approval of the arrangement. In most boats this arrangement consists of a standard marine toilet, plumbed to an approved holding tank. There are a range of ecologically safe systems that use composting and other methods. The approved holding tanks in use comprise polyethylene tanks, or bladder type tanks. The biggest issue for boaters is selecting the right sized tank with regard to people using the system and the time between pump outs. Emptying is usually via a deck fitting and tanks have a vent line and siphon break overboard.

Troubleshooting MSD systems

Always follow the manufacturer's instructions. Normal trouble-shooting principles apply. Check the power supply, check that auto and manual selection is correct, the control system may require a reset. Check inputs and outputs to level switches or solenoids. Operational checks include the following:

Daily. Check macerator pumps, discharge, backwash and sludge pumps and electric motors for unusual noises and vibration. Check all hose and pipe connections for leaks. Make sure the chlorination liquid (bleach) reservoir is full. Check pump pressures are normal where they are installed.

6 Monthly. Check control panel for moisture ingress and corrosion, and ensure cover is closed tightly. Check and tighten all connectors every year. Replace desiccant crystals if installed.

Yearly. Check treatment and sediment tank anodes if installed. Check that solenoid valves are operating correctly, and remove to check and clean. Grease bearings only in accordance with operating hour requirements, typically every 10,000 hours.

About basic toilet systems

While we have looked at MSDs it is important to cover toilets as a separate item. Toilets come either as a manual system, or as an electric unit with integral macerating function. Manual systems use a piston rod type pump to pump out the combined sewage and the flushing seawater. Electric pumps replace the piston rod pump with an impeller type pump and macerator that effectively liquefies waste. These systems use a lot more water to ensure that all materials are flushed out properly.

Figure 9-1 Typical Sewage System
(Courtesy Vetus)

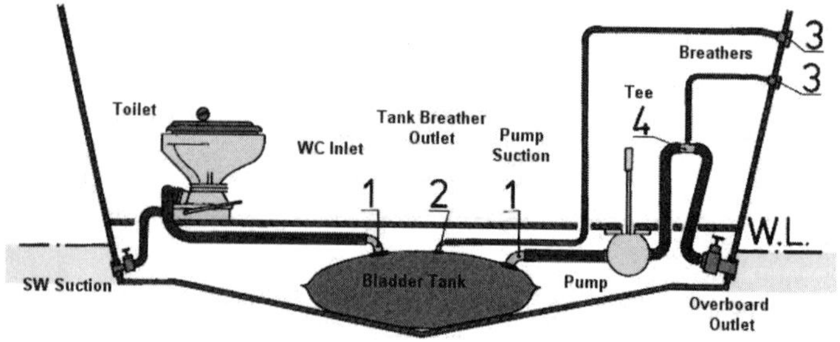

Electric toilets

One of the biggest problems with electric toilets is the failure to install adequately sized cables to the units or allow for voltage drop. The PAR unit consumes 18 amps and requires a heavy-duty cable rated at around 30 amps.

1. As toilets are always located in a wet shower area, ensure that all electrical connections are taped up with water-proof self-amalgamating tapes.

2. Always allow sufficient cable length to pull the toilet out, as it is generally difficult to disconnect the motor.

3. Check the motor connections monthly to ensure no corrosion is occurring. Lightly coat the terminals with silicon or Vaseline.

4. I have started to repaint motors with an additional paint layer to seal and prevent water seeping into the motor housing flanges, as corrosion occurs here easily.

5. Before installation, remove each bolt and apply anti-seize grease.

Toilet waste

It is essential that only normal waste be put through the toilet. To quote that readily available plaque for marine heads, *"Don't put anything in the bowl that you haven't eaten and already digested."* Macerator cutter plates are easily jammed or damaged by putting cigarette and cigar butts, rags and sanitary towels down the bowl. Cleaning macerators is the most unpleasant task on a boat so it is well worth making the effort.

Vacuum toilets

There are many power vessels with vacuum flush, they use small water quantities, and a vacuum pump to operate. These units have vacuum ejector pumps or generators and discharge pumps that require routine inspection and maintenance, along with automatic valves, vacuum and level sensors, and the control system with alarms. 12-volt vacuum pumps have typical power consumptions of 4–6 amps and large boat systems have pumps up to ½ hp. Discharge pumps consume around 6 amps.

Macerator pumps

Macerator pumps are usually connected to the holding tank discharge and are often used to pump out waste to shore facility tanks or overboard. The pumps grind waste to around 3mm size, and are self priming.

It should be remembered that pumps are not rated continuously, and run times should not exceed approximately 10 minutes. Heavy-duty models are available for larger systems and greater pump-out capabilities.

After pumping out tanks, flush out macerator pump with clean water to expel any debris that may cause bacterial build-ups. Use caution when operating; when running dry they will be damaged very quickly.

Troubleshooting macerator pumps

When pumps are noisy, or have low discharge pressures and volumes, or are excessively noisy and have vibration the causes are probably due to the following:

1. The pump or pipes are clogged

2. The pump impeller or cutter is worn

3. The pump has a reduced speed due to wiring and connection faults

4. High viscosity liquids have been used

5. The pump axial clearances have altered

6. The pump bearings are damaged by water ingress

7. The pump has cavitation or a loose impeller.

Holding tanks

Holding tanks need to be able to safely hold waste, either for overboard discharge offshore, or to the shore pump-out station. Tanks require a vent and breather to deck level. As the smell can be strong you can install a filter cartridge. It is recommended that all holding tanks be installed with a tank level indicator or gauge to monitor tank levels. Holding tank odor is always present and a good method of ensuring aerobic bacteria growth is to inject air into the tank so that bacteria thrive and consume waste.

Sewage system hoses

All hoses used in toilet systems need to be high quality reinforced types. The large 1½-inch corrugated hoses with smooth inside bore should be used. Inlet water line hoses of inferior grade are prone to collapse when line is plugged.

1. All joints must be properly double clamped over pump and barbed adaptor fittings to ensure that no material leaks out under pressure.

2. All hoses should be installed so that no material can settle in low points. This is where so-called permeation failure starts. The hoses will start to emit odors from the internal effluent.

Toilet fittings

Seacocks must always be of the highest quality available. In general the flush water uses a ¾ inch reinforced hose, and the overboard is 1½ inch. I use Marelon fittings. The vented loop is absolutely essential on the water inlet and any overboard pump out line. Boat sinkings, caused by siphons in the head overboard discharge line, are common. Always turn off the overboard valves when not using the head. Always use a quality Y-Valve for the tank or overboard selection. Choose one with a center position as it closes off both ports. Also choose one that allows easy locking for USCG inspections.

Overboard pumps

While some boats use a macerator pump the most common is a manual or electrically driven diaphragm pump. They tend to pump without blocking. I prefer the Whale pump units. I also use a Whale Gulper that is able to handle solids up to 1½ inches. In fact I have standardized my onboard pumps on the Whale Gulper series. Always check that the overboard discharge valve is open before starting to pump or you may cause damage that requires a rather unpleasant repair job.

Sewage system maintenance

1. Flush the toilets through regularly. Some recommend dropping down some olive oil to lubricate toilet pump internals. Usually you will get some rather nasty smelling black water come through.

2. Inspect the toilet for leaks, signs of corrosion, and cracks on various components.

3. Check that all hoses are secure and clamped properly. Always use correct sized clamps; I have frequently lacerated my hands, and when contaminated with toilet bacteria it's a nasty wound.

4. Operate all valves several times to ensure they are not seizing up.

5. Rebuild your toilet pump sections every 2 years or so and carry the overhaul kits. It is easier to do in a port than offshore somewhere.

ACKNOWLEDGEMENTS

Thanks and appreciation go to the following companies for their assistance and readers are encouraged to contact them for equipment advice and supply. Quality equipment is part of reliability!

Jabsco	www.jabsco.com
FloJet	www.flojet.com
Rule	www.rule-industries.com
Whale	www.whalepumps.com.
Cleghorn Waring	www.cleghorn.co.uk
SHURFlo	www.shurflo.com
Vetus	www.vetus.com

INDEX

Two practical books for every boater

Marine Diesel Engines
Maintenance and Repair Manual
Jean-Luc Pallas

The book covers the different engine parts and what they do, how the engine propels the boat, simple maintenance tasks, typical problem areas which can lead to a breakdown. Troubleshooting tables to enable you to diagnose the problem and fix it, and how to winterize your engine in your afternoon are also topics covered.

"Pallas explains the basic operation of marine diesel engines and describes essential techniques for their maintenance and repair. Color photographs and diagrams clearly illustrate each step. Most of the tasks described are within the abilities of the average boat owner and require no specialized equipment. Pallas is an instructor of recreational marine mechanics at La Rochelle Technical College in France."
—Sci-Tech Book News

Outboard Motors
Maintenance and Repair Manual
Jean-Luc Pallas

The aim of this book, with its superb step-by-step photographs and detailed diagrams, is to enable every owner to understand the workings of an outboard motor (2 or 4 stroke) and be able to fix it with relative ease.

"This maintenance and repair manual provides everything you need to know about maintaining and fixing outboard engines. Simple maintenance tasks are covered along with problem areas and troubleshooting tables to help you diagnose problems. Step-by-step photographs and detailed diagrams help make it easy."
—Latitudes & Attitudes

America's Favorite Sailing Books
www.sheridanhouse.com